EQUIPPED TO WIN

Seven Strategies for Defeating the Hated Seven

VICTORIA JANTZEN
AND DALTON JANTZEN

WITH

CAROLYN STANFORD GOSS

©2015 by Vicki Jantzen, Dalton Jantzen, and Carolyn Stanford Goss

Unless otherwise noted, Bible passages in this book are from the Holy Bible, English Standard Version® (ESV), copyright © 2001 by Crossway, a publishing ministry of Good News Publishers. ESV® Text Edition: 2011.

The Holy Bible, English Standard Version (ESV) is adapted from the Revised Standard Version of the Bible, copyright Division of Christian Education of the National Council of the Churches of Christ in the U.S.A. All rights reserved.

The "ESV" and "English Standard Version" are trademarks of Good News Publishers. Use of either trademark requires the permission of Good News Publishers.

Verses noted as NIV are from THE HOLY BIBLE, NEW INTERNATIONAL VERSION®, NIV® Copyright © 1973, 1978, 1984, 2011 by Biblica, Inc.® Used by permission. All rights reserved worldwide.

Scripture noted as NKJV is taken from the New King James Version®. Copyright © 1982 by Thomas Nelson. Used by permission. All rights reserved.

Other Publications by Dalton Jantzen or Vicki Jantzen:

The Spiritually Healthy Leader, a 6-workbook series available in English, Spanish, Russian, and Nepalese

The Cultivator, a monthly publication in English and Spanish

Faces of The BACK 40, reports about Christian leaders in countries other than the United States.

Contents

Prologue:
God's Truth Shows Up in the Most Surprising Places 1

Introduction:
Get Your Gear Ready..11

Chapter 1:
The Mind is a Terrible Thing to Leave Vulnerable..........21

Chapter 2:
My Hands Are Full and That's a Good Thing 29

Chapter 3:
Follow Your Heart or Guard Your Heart? 37

Chapter 4:
Do You Wear Slip-ons or Tie-ons?.................................49

Chapter 5:
Live a Lie or Live the Truth? 59

Chapter 6:
Stir Up or Build Up? Putting Your Prayer On................69

Chapter 7:
Equipped to Win—Love Conquers Hate 79

A Note About 30 60 100 Ministries 91

About the Authors 93

End Notes 97

PROLOGUE
God's Truth Shows Up in the Most Surprising Places

THE YEAR WAS 1897, during one of the last two gold rushes in the American territories. Having exhausted most of the California gold rush opportunities, hundreds of adventurous men and a few enterprising women trekked to the frozen land and lakes of the Klondike in Yukon Territory. If they were hardy enough to make the arduous climb up the Chilkoot Pass en route to Dawson, they became obsessed with finding that one Bonanza that would make them rich. An occasional con man or preacher or madam completed the pop-up towns that grew overnight.

While some of these new residents may have followed traditional morals and ethics in their previous homes, when they arrived in the harsh conditions of the wilderness, they often set aside conventional ideas of right and wrong. They sometimes, some of them oftentimes, stole, cheated and even killed. Some admittedly committed these crimes for pleasure, but many were desperate for necessities such as firewood to keep them warm one more night or food to stave off the hunger pangs for a couple days. And some of the women, with few options, relied on selling themselves.

The numbers of lost, hurting, and hungry people created a new opportunity for men of God to sacrifice the comforts of the lower continent in order to do what they could to preserve civilization and morality.

The TV miniseries *Klondike* tells a story based on historical fact and real people, and at the same time it offers a rich vein of truth about human nature. As I watched the film portraying the prospectors searching for gold and the evils lurking around every cabin, my mind went on a search of its own.

One scene registered with me in a powerful way. A beautiful prostitute named Sabine is humiliated in the middle of the muddy Main Street by a rich man who taunts her by throwing money at her and daring her to strip. A local businesswoman rescues her and takes her to Dawson City's church for refuge.

The next day she asks the preacher, Father Judge, what she, as a prostitute, can do to live a better life. He begins to tell her about love, the kind that drives out fear as he places his hands on her head and then moves to her chest. Immediately I thought, OK, here we go, the typical film portrayal of a lustful preacher—you talk about love and then take advantage of her—for after all, she's just a prostitute.[1] I fully expected him to show his true nature and reveal what a hypocrite he was as he laid hands on her in inappropriate places.

When that did not happen, I was pleased to see that he resisted any temptation that he might have felt. Maybe he realized the Enemy's plan was to challenge him with numerous temptations in order to discourage and defeat him, and he needed to be prepared for any onslaught of the Enemy.

Then I remembered how, as a child in Sunday School we learned about the armor of God and how it helps us fight temptation. We would use our hands to 'put "the helmet of salvation" on our head and then the "breastplate of righteousness" on our chest, and so on, and the correlation between sin and the armor of God hit me like a mother lode.

In *Klondike* the preacher stays faithful to his calling. He does not do anything dishonorable to Sabine, nor does the script have him capitulating to the Hollywood stereotype. Father Judge's portrayal is based on fact—history tells us he remained a man of God the people of the town dubbed "the Saint of Dawson." How encouraging that is to know!

God spoke to me through this scene in the miniseries *Klondike*, and inspired me to read Proverbs 6 and the list of the seven things God hates, and then on to Ephesians 6, which lists the pieces of the armor of God that we as believers can use to battle those seven things.

Interesting Story . . . But What Does It Have to Do with My Life?

It has everything to do with you.

The writer of Proverbs wrote the words God gave him several centuries before Christ, and yet, they still ring true. Individuals who moved to the harsh climate of Dawson City exhibited many of them. But the conditions there did not bring them on; they only made them more recognizable.

Ask yourself whether the seven things the Lord hates from Proverbs 6:16-19 seem familiar today, as well:

> *There are six things that the Lord hates,*
> *seven that are an abomination to him:*
> *haughty eyes, a lying tongue,*
> *and hands that shed innocent blood,*
> *a heart that devises wicked plans,*
> *feet that make haste to run to evil,*
> *a false witness who breathes out lies,*
> *and one who sows discord among brothers.*
> —English Standard Version

Other Bible translations convey the same truth in slightly different words. The one below is from the New International Version, and it uses language that may be easier for us twenty-first century believers to understand:

> *There are six things the Lord hates,*
> *seven that are detestable to him:*
> *haughty eyes, a lying tongue,*
> *hands that shed innocent blood,*
> *a heart that devises wicked schemes,*
> *feet that are quick to rush into evil,*
> *a false witness who pours out lies*
> *and a person who*
> *stirs up conflict in the community.*

Can you say you have never encountered people that model these self-centered and destructive traits?

Are you brave enough to include yourself?

Prologue

Maybe you have been a victim of the types of behaviors these traits bring forward and that the Klondike miniseries portrays. Maybe the uncomfortable truth is that you recognize yourself in one or more of the seven things God hates.

Have we become more compassionate and less selfish as we become more educated and have increased our standard of living? Reality suggests otherwise. The issues that plague us today—war, hunger, disease, human-caused environmental disasters, and others, are as old as history. So are crimes caused by jealousy, greed, and other poisonous emotions. Men and women back to the first humans confronted the same dangers, and they are the same ones that raised their ugly heads in the town of Dawson City during its Gold Rush Days. They are the same ones that caused your coworker to bad mouth you or a neighbor to pass gossip about you around the neighborhood.

We have learned ways to survive and to use our resources in ways that people long ago would have never even conceived, and our progress in living standards can make us think we are more advanced than people were in the past. Yet we have not improved much in our relationships with our fellow humans. Think about these numbers:

- Worldwide, 11.7 percent of the world's population is at war.[2]

- American divorce rates are at 40 to 50 percent.[3]

- The Census Bureau estimates food-insecure households in the US at 14.3 percent.[4]

- Compassion International estimates that worldwide 600 million children are living in extreme poverty.[5]

It seems we have a long way to go before we can practice the directive of the apostle Paul:

> *Do nothing from selfish ambition or conceit, but in humility count others more significant than yourselves.*
> —Philippians 2:3

Perhaps people in the church's early days had self-serving attitudes that weren't much different from ours. Why else would Paul have focused on such attitudes? Did the men who went prospecting for gold in 1897 do so out of a desire to make the world a better place? History records that they were so bent on making a fortune in gold in the Klondike that they would steal and kill to get what they wanted.

Another stark statistic produces another question: Public records show that CEOs today in some cases make as much as 800 times more than the people who work for them.[6]

Do these figures indicate we have become more unselfish?

Again you may be asking, what does this have to do with me?

Again, I answer, "Everything."

The Enemy uses The Hated Seven to cut off intimacy with God so that we are not victorious in our Christian life.

We hope you will take time to learn about the ones

that are actually hateful to God so you will recognize and deal with them when they threaten you.

Some Suggested Uses for This Book

Individual Study

People these days are so busy! It's often difficult to justify getting up an extra fifteen minutes earlier than you usually do to spend personal time with the Lord. If you are not a morning person, perhaps you will pick up *Equipped to Win: Seven Strategies for Defeating the Hated Seven* when you are on your lunch hour or after you eat dinner in the evening. The time of day is not as important as developing the habit of regularly spending time with God. If your desire is to cultivate a vibrant personal relationship with God, this book is a great way to start.

Equipped to Win's chapters are short and the entire book is brief. We hope you will find time to fit it into your schedule because its theme, how we can be victorious in spiritual warfare, is key to your growth and maturity in Christ.

With a Friend

You may be familiar with the fact that only a diamond can cut another diamond. When the jeweler uses a diamond to cut the light-splitting facets in the raw rock, his work makes it sparkle. So it is with a mutual agreement to read *Equipped to Win* with a partner. Set aside fifteen to twenty minutes each week to discuss the truths in each chapter one by one and then pray with each other for a few minutes. Your keeping each other accountable will help clarify points you each may have questions about and highlight new facets of Proverbs 6:16-19 and Ephesians 6:13-18 that you may not have seen before.

Group Study

Would you like to ratchet up your regular meetings over coffee with a group of friends? *Equipped to Win* lends itself well to small groups because it is a relatively short-term commitment. It is easy to understand and yet raises one of the most important steps toward maturity a Christian can take: Successfully fighting off the assaults of the world, the flesh, and the Enemy, not all at once but one battle at a time.

You might think of other groups, as well. The most obvious is the Sunday School class. This book would lend itself to the short modules many churches have adopted in which the class studies a subject for 6-8 weeks.

However you choose to read and absorb this book, our wish and prayer is that you engage with it—that you examine yourself, ask yourself questions about your own spiritual battles, and then listen to the Holy Spirit's still, small voice showing you where and when you need to put God's armor to use. It only awaits your picking it up, putting it on, and being confident that you, or rather God in you, will win. In fact, you have already won! Believe it! Embrace it!

Notes

INTRODUCTION
Get Your Gear Ready

- "I detest eggplant."
- "I detest reality TV."
- "I detest having to shovel snow."

Does the word *detest* seem a bit strong to you in these contexts? Maybe it should when we consider its meaning:

> *Detest (verb): to feel intense and often violent antipathy toward: loathe, hate*
> *Detestable (adjective): arousing or meriting intense dislike; abominable**
> —Merriam-Webster's 11th Collegiate Dictionary

(* italics in definition are mine)

Think of the statements above and look at the dictionary definition. Does the word *detest* still apply? Maybe it does for you! If so, you must really hate eggplant, reality TV, and shoveling snow!

But do you feel violent antipathy toward them? (*Webster's* defines antipathy as "settled aversion or dislike, distaste"—strong words, indeed.) Are they an *abomination* to you? Would you throw the eggplant down on the floor and stomp on it to show your rage if someone served it to you? Would you go get a gun and shoot the TV screen if you happened to turn on the remote and it landed on *Survivor* or *The Bachelor* or a similar show? Would you throw the shovel up in the air and hope it lands broken the next time you see a few fresh inches outside?

People use *detest* or its synonyms *loathe* and *hate* when another word or phrase might be less of an exaggeration and more accurate: "I don't like the taste of eggplant," "I find reality TV a waste of my free time," "Shoveling snow off the driveway tires me out." Some of us tend to exaggerate our feelings at times. Do you?

There are cases when God speaks, though, where he uses these words in ways that can hardly be stronger than they are. Consider this statement again:

> *There are six things the LORD hates,*
> *seven that are an abomination to him.*
> —Proverbs 6:16

In the Bible, when the writer uses the words that a translator translates into English as "hate," "despise," or "abomination," there is a reason for choosing the word—it most accurately portrays the intensity of God's feelings about sin.

The term describing God's hate towards these sins, *saanee*, is one used in Hebrew for "foe." In other words, God views what I will call "The Hated Seven" as an enemy . . . a word picture that gives pause. An enemy?

Introduction

Who wants to behave in such a way as to spark a war with the Creator of the universe? Not us as believers.

The truth is that it is not God we want to fight, and it is not people. It is not, in the apostle Paul's word, a battle against "flesh and blood." Rather, we battle "against the cosmic powers over this present darkness, against the spiritual forces of evil in the heavenly places" (Ephesians 6:12, from a passage we will discuss in more detail in later pages).

That thought can be enough to shake even the most complacent Christ-follower from a sluggish, self-satisfied slumber and into spiritually healthy combat. God goes on to trace The Hated Seven visually, starting at the top of the human body and moving down: haughty eyes, a lying tongue, hands that kill, a conniving heart, feet that rush into evil, a false witness, and a man who stirs up discord among the brothers.

"I know someone who is the perfect example of (insert characteristic)." That might be our first reaction when we are confronted with these seven things that are an abomination to God. Interesting how when thinking of a negative personality trait, one tends to designate someone else as an example of the attitude or behavior.

Maybe the tendency to see faults in others but not in ourselves is why when Jesus preached to the people of Jerusalem on a mountainside, he rhetorically asked, "Why do you see the speck that is in your brother's eye, but do not notice the log that is in your own eye? (Matthew 7:3).

Is Jesus' question one that applies to human nature, or what? Even as creatures being made new in Christ, our old sin nature tries to surface from time to time. We may find ourselves being judgmental toward others. As we become more mature in our faith, we may realize that we, too, have tendencies to portray the seven things God hates, and we want to fight them off.

So what do we do?

How can we arm ourselves against the temptation to have haughty eyes, a lying tongue, and the temptation to practice the other abominable sins?

Well. . . God has given us the armor to protect ourselves against our old nature and from the evil influences of the world around us. As always, God connects the dots, providing another head-to-toe word picture painted by the apostle Paul that enables us to "see" how his protection kicks in, and in fact, is always with us, awaiting our picking it up and putting it on.

Putting on the Armor

In the New Testament book of Ephesians 6:13-18 we find a list of separate pieces of spiritual armor that together make up a kit of practical tools we can use to battle The Hated Seven.

> *Therefore take up the whole armor of God, that you may be able to withstand in the evil day, and having done all, to stand firm. Stand therefore, having fastened on the belt of truth, and having put on the breastplate of righteousness, and, as shoes for your feet, having put on the readiness given by the gospel of peace. In all circumstances take up the shield of faith, with which you can extinguish all the flaming darts of the evil one; and take the helmet of salvation,*

Introduction

and the sword of the Spirit, which is the word of God, praying at all times in the Spirit, with all prayer and supplication. To that end keep alert with all perseverance, making supplication for all the saints.

Belt . . . breastplate . . . shoes . . . shield . . . helmet . . . sword . . . prayer. What? How is prayer in the same category as the other pieces? This book will answer that question as it traces how to use each piece of our gear each day and what the value of each piece is.

Realizing What We're Up Against

First things first. There are some truths you need to know about battling The Hated Seven.

1. God doesn't hate you. He hates sin.

Have you ever heard the saying, "Hate the sin but not the sinner?" We should be aware that some attitudes and actions are, quite simply, wrong, and because we know from experience how humans can fall off the straight path, we should hate the actions or attitudes but forgive the perpetrator. Forgiving does not mean excusing the perpetrator's bad behavior with attitudes such as "Boys will be boys" or "She just has a surplus of energy." We recognize sin—but we forgive as God has forgiven us.

God's battle with sin is unique only to Him. God is holy, sinless, spotless, flawless. If he weren't God, we might wonder how he even knows what sin is, since sin is foreign to him. If your native language is anything but Chinese or Farsi, think of yourself seeing text written in Chinese or Farsi for the first time. Unless you had earlier learned the Chinese or Farsi alphabets, you would have no context for reading either one.

God is God, though, and being all-knowing, what Christians have historically called omniscient, he sees not just the current picture but the total picture. Though sinless, He knows what sin is. He has given us the ability to choose whether to go our own way or not and he knows the consequences of the way we choose to live. He is the originator of what we call "free will," the ability to decide whether we will follow our own way or God's way. Understand the difference between God's view of sin and ours: God loves us deeply, but he doesn't love everything we do. If we're honest, we detest plenty of things we do, too. That puts us in good company . . . with God.

2. God equips you.

How gracious our God is to provide a set of gear he has specially designed to battle The Hated Seven! He lists protective gear for each area of our bodies: a helmet for our head, a breastplate for our heart, a shield for our protection, a belt around our torso, a sword for our arms, and shoes for our feet. God gives us everything we need to wage this daily battle.

Think about it: These are not just defensive items. They arm the Christ-follower for action. Shoes walk, jump, skip, and run. They allow us to move into active combat with the Enemy, not just follow behind our leader or hide behind a bush. We know we are equipped, outfitted in God's protective armor.

3. God wants you to win.

In the set of instructions Paul gives as he lists the armor of God, he uses the verb *stand* three times in just one-and-a-half verses: "Therefore take up the whole armor of God, that you may be able to with*stand* in the evil day, and having done all, to *stand* firm. *Stand* therefore . . ." (Ephesians 6:13-14a, italics mine).

The ability to stand is both defensive and offensive. God's armor, when used according to His instructions, allows us to play defense against The Hated Seven—to withstand or stand against challenges and to oppose them. Yet the armor allows us to play offense, too, in the ability to press on and continue in our purpose. "If God is for us, who can be against us?" (Romans 8:31).

The Hated Seven are deadly. When we're spiritually healthy, they are poised for attack every day. God is on our side, working with each of us day by day, minute by minute, pulling for us to win. And we will.

All he asks is for us to get our gear ready . . . and then use it.

God's Battle Plan: Growth Point

God equips you to be vigilant. What does the word *vigilant* mean to you? We often hear the word *vigil* when a group holds a candlelight prayer service or a continuous remembrance service for a person who is missing or who died unexpectedly in a car accident, during the commission of a crime, and other instances. How can you be vigilant?

God's Reinforcements: Scripture

> *Therefore take up the whole armor of God, that you may be able to withstand in the evil day, and having done all, to stand firm.*
> —Ephesians 6:13

God's Battle Strategy: Prayer Points

- Sins that hurt others are particularly detestable to God. Why? Ask God to make you sensitive to the ways you hurt others—not necessarily in a physical way but through your words and actions.

- When it comes to our natural tendencies, what is the difference between playing defense and playing offense?

- Why is personal vigilance the mark of a spiritually healthy Christ-follower?

Notes

CHAPTER 1
The Mind is a Terrible Thing to Leave Vulnerable

AS YOU DRIVE down the highway, do you ever see people on motorcycles speeding in and out of vehicles and wearing no helmet? Do you see children without protective gear riding their bicycles on streets in your neighborhood? A friend of mine says her grandchildren are horrified if she rides her bicycle without a helmet!

Why is a helmet an important piece of protective gear? According to one well-known emergency room physician, non-helmeted riders are 14 times more likely to be involved in a fatal crash from head injuries.[7] Because the brain directs both our thoughts and our most basic actions, a person with a brain injury can end up dependent upon others for the most basic needs for the rest of his or her life.

As we think of the believer's battle gear and work systematically downward from head to feet in our mental picture of the battle-ready Christian, we note that Ephesians 6:17 advises the believer to wear "the helmet of salvation." Let's take a look at why the helmet of salvation is so key to arming ourselves against The Hated Seven.

What is the Helmet of Salvation?

This piece of armor has two components to consider: 1) the helmet itself and 2) why it is closely associated with salvation. A helmet is a hard, sometimes padded hat that fits tightly around one's head, encircling it and protecting it. Think of a bike helmet, military helmet, or football helmet.

Likewise, a spiritual helmet is God's way of protecting the parts of our head: our mind (what we think and believe as revealed in our thought life), our eyes (what we choose to see as revealed in how we look at ourselves and others), and our tongue (what we think as revealed in what we say.) Note the common theme. The helmet protects *what we think* and is crucial to the renewing of our minds as believers, as Paul counsels us in Romans 12:2:

> *Do not be conformed to this world, but be transformed by the renewal of your mind, that by testing you may discern what is the will of God, what is good and acceptable and perfect.*

We are new creations in Christ (2 Corinthians 5:17), but we know that a shiny new object—a bicycle, a car, a shovel, a watch, and so on—becomes less useful with neglect. We can see the results: it gets rusty and weak. We must take care of our tools, for regular maintenance can improve their performance.

Similarly, we must take care of our helmet of salvation, God's gift to us through the death and resurrection of Jesus. It is of highest value and deserves respect.

Chapter 1

It will protect us and rescue us from our sin and its consequences. Put another way, salvation delivers us from believing and embracing lies. It reveals the truth to our minds.

Connecting the two components together, we can understand that the helmet of salvation serves to protect and rescue our minds—and consequently our eyes and tongues—from the lies of sin and their consequences.

But we must put it on.

How Do the Eyes and Tongue Get in So Much Trouble?

A recent American comedy show often described someone giving someone else "the stink eye" when a person wanted to make another person feel uncomfortable. Think about that term—it's a good way to portray the poisonous looks that originate in pride.

Haughty eyes (Proverbs 6:17) are a reflection of pride. Pride begins with those thoughts that believe in and rely on our superior accomplishments, abilities, position, possessions, talents, and resources.

A lying tongue, on the other hand, is one that deceives, disappoints, or betrays not just others, but often ourselves, too. Our words reveal lies that disguise themselves as thoughts. If we don't put on the helmet of salvation, those thoughts will not have the protection they need. They will become toxic, cynical, and critical, and influence what comes out of our mouths.

A haughty look and a lying tongue are two separate modes of operation, yet both reveal what we think. Proud looks and deceptive words originate in our minds and then grow, much as a small lump of dough rises with yeast's action to fill a large bowl.

If we choose to listen to thoughts spoken by the Enemy, he can fill our minds with lies and direct our emotions, controlling our points of view and our words.

We must keep that helmet of salvation securely on through regular maintenance: prayer, meditation, reading of God's Word, and actions of love toward our neighbor.

Take the Helmet Each Day

Some of us only think of salvation as a one-time event, but its ongoing process is one of regeneration.

Ephesians 6:17 says, "Take the helmet of salvation." The term *take* means to receive; to accept. Think of it as similar to the Spanish verb *tomar*, which means "to drink or to take." When we take a glass of water, we don't just pour it on the ground. We use it as a tool to quench our thirst. When we take the helmet of salvation and place it on our head, we receive and accept God's protection for our mind, and thus, for our eyes and tongue, and we make use of that protection.

God knows that the helmet of salvation is a piece of armor that will protect our mind from lies, thereby keeping our eyes and tongue from evil. He offers us the helmet of salvation each day.

But in order to have that protection, we must choose to put it on and put it to work.

Each day.

Chapter 1

God's Battle Plan: Growth Point

Proud looks and deceptive words originate in our minds—as thoughts. They may often seem as if they "just happen," but they do not. How can we guard those thoughts as we wear the helmet of salvation?

God's Reinforcements: Scripture

Take the helmet of salvation.
—Ephesians 6:17

God's Battle Strategy: Prayer Points

- Examine your thoughts and ask God to show you how you may inadvertently give place to pride in your abilities, position, or possessions.

- Consider a time when your thoughts may have led you to deceive another person or yourself. Ask forgiveness from God for that time, and if appropriate, ask the person you hurt for forgiveness, too.

- Who is your salvation—and what has that salvation done for you in your life? Offer praise to God for His gift to you.

- What can you do to remember to put on your helmet of salvation each day?

Notes

CHAPTER 2
My Hands Are Full, and That's a Good Thing

IN THE *KLONDIKE* miniseries that first started my reflections on The Hated Seven, adventurer and gold prospector Bill Haskell's best friend and fellow prospector Byron Epstein is murdered early in the story. Determined to find and capture the killer, Bill arms himself and waits for the murderer to reveal himself. He knows the killer is vicious, so Bill keeps his weapon ready, though it takes a long time for the killer to reveal himself.

Bill is what people in some parts of the US call "loaded for bear." Just as no one would take a toy bow and arrow to a bear hunt, Bill keeps a gun at the ready that is powerful enough to kill a killer. So it is with the weapons a believer carries in order to arm oneself against the onslaughts from The Hated Seven. Resistance against The Hated Seven sins is not a child's pretend game—and the weapons God provides equip us to be victorious.

We know that Proverbs 6:16-19 starts at the top of the human body and moves down: haughty eyes, a lying tongue, hands that kill, a conniving heart, feet that rush into evil, a false witness, and a man who stirs up discord.

God does not tell us that He hates it when we act a

certain way or when we commit The Hated Seven sins without providing every powerful piece of armor we need to resist and overcome the temptation to manifest that behavior. So in Ephesians 6:13-18, God provides a set of practical tools we can use to battle those seven sins, which include the belt of truth, the breastplate of righteousness, shoes shod with the gospel of peace, the shield of faith, the helmet of salvation, the sword of the Spirit, and prayer.

That word picture—that description of the various pieces of protective gear a soldier equipped for battle would wear—shows that being properly prepared involves more than merely providing protection for your body. A well-dressed Christ-follower's hands are full, not empty. They hold the sword of the Spirit, poised for active engagement, and the shield of faith, which protects from all potentially deadly influences.

Are Your Hands Idle – or Occupied?

Have you ever considered the possibility that your hands can shed innocent blood? (Proverbs 6:17)

The original word for *hand* in Proverbs 6:17 ("hands that sheds innocent blood") indicates a hand that is open, rather than closed. Open hands are unoccupied and more apt to find trouble. They may move from inactivity into action—and then the hands become instruments that damage and destroy.

In contrast, busy hands are useful, provided they are holding the right tools.

Chapter 2

What Is in Your Hands?

Ephesians 6:16-17 tells us to "take the shield of faith and the sword of the Spirit, which is the Word of God." When your hands grasp firmly onto God's weapons, you are ready to both attack and defend. Yet your battle is not against people. God clearly tells us that we must use his weapons against evil forces in the spiritual world:

> *For we do not wrestle against flesh and blood, but against the rulers, against the authorities, against the cosmic powers over this present darkness, against the spiritual forces of evil in the heavenly places.*
> —Ephesians 6:12

The Sword of the Spirit

Without God's Word in your hands, you can face two dangerous problems. You may attack the wrong opponent—another person, for example, rather than the Enemy. Without the discernment God's Word teaches you as you study it and meditate upon it, you can shed innocent blood. In other words, you can use your words to hurt people. The children's rhyme that states "Words can never hurt me" is wrong, isn't it?

You can be more destructive than you realize: your words may not destroy a person physically, but they can be emotionally, mentally, and spiritually destructive. When you have been on the receiving end of hurtful words, you have probably found they can pierce your soul like a lance and without God's help the damage is often irreversible.

The second danger is that you may use your own words, thoughts, and beliefs rather than the Truth—and I capitalize the word truth purposely when I refer to the Bible. You may be too tolerant. "Anything Goes" might be a cute song title, but for the Christian, anything does not go. Ignorance of and disregard for God's Word has allowed many practices that do not honor the God we worship and that do not comply with His will.

Human words may not be truth and can bring harm to others. The sword of the Spirit is the Word of God. The Word of God reveals the truth about our destructive tendencies. It can show us how to build up others rather than tear them down. The Word of God can also bring healing when we are wounded.

When your hands hold firmly to God's Word, He directs you in how to use His truth in the most skillful way to discern your true Enemy and to understand specific situations you face. God's Word is a strong, reliable weapon, and it can go on the offense if the situation calls for it.

The Shield of Faith

We think of a shield as a defensive tool, but Paul uses a word for *faith* that refers to more than simple defense. Here are some definitions of *pistis,* the Greek word Paul uses:

- Refers to a conviction that something is true.

- Relates to the Christ-follower's trust and belief regarding his relationship to God and divine things.

- Suggests holy fervor.

The last point may be the most important one. "Fervor" is a word we do not hear much these days. What is it?

According to the dictionary, "fervor" is active and expressive. It is bold. It does not merely hide behind a safe barrier. Think of the shield of faith in this way: It is defensive, but it equips us to move forward.

The shield of faith quenches fiery darts—those tricks, temptations, annoyances, and lies that the Enemy uses to wound or distract you and put you out of commission, even temporarily. Faith is crucial as we face the destructive side of doubt. The shield of faith gives us protection so we can move forward, not just set up our camp in place and wait for the enemy to attack us.

The term used for *shield* indicates a very large piece of equipment shaped like a door. A door! A door-sized shield would offer cover to your entire body as you battle the onslaughts of the Enemy. Your shield of faith is big enough and powerful enough to cover any situation you face, provided it is in your hands and you use it.

Use What's in Your Hands

When your hands take up a sword and a shield each day, you will not focus on issues that do not matter, nor will you have time to harm others. As you practice putting on this armor every day, you will learn to say, as Paul did, "None of these things move me" (Acts 20:24 NKJV).

Instead, your hands will be full. Your eyes will be trained on the real Enemy. And you will fight him using no-fail spiritual gear.

God's Battle Plan: Growth Point

Make it a point to keep your hands and thoughts occupied with the Word of God and the shield of faith.

God's Reinforcements: Scripture

> *Take up the shield of faith, with which you can extinguish all the flaming arrows of the evil one . . . and the sword of the Spirit, which is the word of God.*
> —Ephesians 6:16-17, NIV

God's Battle Strategy: Prayer Points

- Think of a time when your words, spoken in the flesh, may have wounded another. Ask God for forgiveness for that time, and then ask Him to show you how and when to ask forgiveness of that person.

- How does the Enemy distract you?

- What is one step you can make today to take up the shield of faith and the sword of the Spirit, the Word of God?

Notes

CHAPTER 3
Follow Your Heart or Guard Your Heart?

IN THE MINISERIES *Klondike*, two characters in the rugged town of Dawson City are instantly recognizable as evil schemers:

- The first is a land grabber who goes by the title, no doubt made up by himself, of "The Count." He cheats, robs, humiliates, and even kills people who stand in the way of his evil plans. The land grabber's heart is so evil that he takes pleasure in humiliating the prostitute in front of a crowd of onlookers, throwing coins at her in the middle of a muddy street and shouting insults.

- The second is a con man who masks his fraudulent operations by acting like the friendly guy who just wants to offer his customers a good deal.

These two incorrigibles are deliberate in their actions, and act upon well thought-out plans—our laws today would say they act "with malice aforethought." It doesn't take much searching to identify people and groups in the news today who have a similar agenda. Their hearts are full of wicked plans, one of The Hated Seven characteristics identified in Proverbs 6:16-19.

> *There are six things that the Lord hates,*
> *seven that are an abomination to him:*
> *haughty eyes, a lying tongue,*
> *and hands that shed innocent blood,*
> *a heart that devises wicked plans,*
> *feet that make haste to run to evil,*
> *a false witness who breathes out lies,*
> *and one who sows discord among brothers.*

What made the hearts of these men so black? Are we all in danger of turning to evil and conniving ways? Are we hopelessly doomed to follow their example? To answer that question, let's start by identifying what we mean when we use the word *heart*.

True or False? "I Love You with All My Heart."

Have you ever said that to someone, or has someone said that to you? When someone uses the words "with all my heart," what does the phrase mean to you?

We can probably agree that it does not mean you are literally handing someone the rhythmically pumping major organ that keeps your blood circulating throughout your body.

Perhaps you have heard *heart* used to refer to your

Chapter 3

intellect, emotion, and will. If you look up *heart* in a dictionary, you will probably find definitions such as "personality," "disposition," "compassionate nature," or "innermost feelings": "She has a good heart."

You may also find *heart* as a way to describe courage or single-minded focus: "He ran the race with all his heart," or "She gave her whole heart to the cause of freedom."

In fact, we use *heart* in our everyday conversation almost without thinking what it means because—to use the word itself—the meanings of the word are close to our hearts.

In Bible times, the term "heart" had a much broader meaning than it does today. While we often separate a person's mind from his feelings, the ancient concept of heart included both—and more.

In Scripture, the heart refers to the totality of all our inner selves, from thinking to feeling to decision-making to the will to the personality. The word *heart* means everything about us that makes us "us"! So if our heart is not protected and governed by the Holy Spirit, we are likely to commit one or more of The Hated Seven, because everything about the totality of our inner selves is vulnerable to attack.

The heart influences our behavior. When left to its own choices and devices it will lead to evil decisions and bad behavior. Deceitful schemes are rooted in the heart. Wicked imaginations are a contrivance. You have to *exert yourself* to plan cleverly or ingeniously invent the scenario that dictates your behavior.

It's an intentional choice—a plan that begins internally, and then moves outwardly. When Jesus preached his Sermon on the Mount he taught his listeners this wise and sober truth that is as true today as it was then: "The good person out of the good treasure of his heart produces good, and the evil person out of the evil treasure produces evil, for out of the abundance of his heart his mouth speaks" (Luke 6:45).

Listening only to our heart often leads to great evil. There is a remedy, though. In Ephesians 6:14 God gives us the antidote to the temptation to listen to our heart when devising the wicked schemes it is prone to concoct, and that Proverbs 6:18 says God hates: "Stand therefore, having fastened on the belt of truth, and having put on the breastplate of righteousness . . ."

The Antidote

God offers us an antidote for the hated sin of thinking up wicked schemes. It is the breastplate of righteousness, which covers and protects us from the temptation to believe our own choices and judgments based on what our unprotected heart tells us. When we have it on, it is a "governor" to our behavior—a reminder to do good and not evil.

We desperately need this protection, for the heart is not just the muscle that controls our physical well-being. More importantly, it is the seat of our emotional and spiritual health and needs the forgiveness and justification offered through the death and resurrection of Jesus Christ. And that protection is provided us when we put on the breastplate of righteousness. Let us consider how it works.

Chapter 3

Righteousness – What Does This Mean?

Righteousness is a word we don't hear much anymore and that's too bad. It is a word that represents the great gift we received as a result of Christ's death and resurrection.

The word *righteousness* comes from the Greek *dikaios*, which means "equitable, just, and by implication innocent or holy." In law, *equity* is a system that supplements the common law and allows flexibility in cases where strict application of the law would result in hardship or unfairness. Interesting how this gives us a picture of grace—as an alternative to the strict application of the law.

We are not righteous nor can we even pretend to be. No matter how hard we try, whatever we do by our own effort is *self*-righteousness. But Jesus was righteous. Because he was innocent, without sin, and knew no sin, his death was a just substitute for our own. Jesus Christ gave those who accept it the gift of righteousness—the declaration of innocence and freedom from guilt and sin—by his sinless death. We are righteous not because we are not guilty of sin, but because God through Jesus has given us this gift of innocence.

That is why it is so important to put on the breastplate of righteousness. Think about this: If we relied on our own righteousness and got what we deserved, we would be condemned to death. But by putting on the breastplate of the righteousness of Christ, the sinless One, we get what *he* deserves—life everlasting.

"Just Follow Your Heart." Should You?

"Follow your heart." How wonderful and inspiring those words sound. The sentiment behind them motivated the two young men in the *Klondike* miniseries to leave behind their comfortable lives in the continental United States and trek first by railroad and then on foot to one of the most inhospitable places in the known world. They went to find the gold that would make them rich. Following their hearts led them to adventure, but it also led them to hardship and death.

"Follow your heart." The late Steve Jobs, founder of Apple, has offered this advice to listeners at many conferences. Oprah Winfrey has said words such as these too many times to count. If you look up "Follow your heart" online, you will find quotations from several hundred famous persons that incorporate this advice. Perhaps you have even received this advice from a family member, friend, spouse, or counselor.

The problems with this advice become obvious. Think of persons you know. Perhaps you have heard someone say their marriage is stagnant so they are going to follow their heart and leave their spouse for a younger, "newer" model. Or maybe you know someone who has left a job or profession to travel around the world to "find himself and follow his heart."

Ask yourself what is wrong with these examples. Would you agree they reveal some self-centeredness? We might say they suggest the person who has said them is not controlling or guarding his or her heart, but is letting it control him.

God hates "a heart that devises wicked plans," what the NIV similarly calls a "conniving heart." When we rely on our own thinking and decisions without wearing God's protective armor, we are very likely to devise a wicked plan. Why wicked? Because it's our plan, not God's. And the human heart is incapable on its own of innocent and pure choices. Hear God's truth from an Old Testament prophet:

> *The heart is deceitful above all things, and desperately sick. Who can understand it?*
> —Jeremiah 17:9

"Wicked plans" (Proverbs 6:18) are intentional decisions we make apart from the Holy Spirit's influence. When left to its own devices, your heart connives plots of its own design rather than God's, placing its decisions squarely into the "wicked schemes" camp.

So when someone advises you to "just follow your heart," take notice. You are being tempted to accept deception, acting on your own version of what is right.

Unless you put on the breastplate of righteousness.

What Is the Breastplate of Righteousness?

In ancient times, the breastplate was a close-fitting piece of armor worn as an undergarment covering the upper part of the body. It protected the vital organs from the waist up—in particular, the heart.

As a piece of spiritual armor, the breastplate protects the heart from its own choices. Self-righteousness is unholy, and an unrestrained heart devises wicked schemes, calling them "justice" and acting out of selfishness or vengeance. When your heart is protected by the breastplate of righteousness, what several modern Bible translations call "right living," it acts by the Holy Spirit's direction. It will lead you to think, feel, decide, and act in right standing with God.

Think of it as a bulletproof vest for your inner soul. We know that by merely trying to be good on our own we will fail—an experience we can all relate to. That is the bad news.

But the good news so outweighs our human limitations! Romans 3:24-25 says we are "justified freely by his grace through the redemption that came by Christ Jesus. God presented Christ as a sacrifice of atonement through the shedding of his blood—to be received by faith. He did this to demonstrate his righteousness . . ."

God freely offers us *his own righteousness* through the death and resurrection of his Son. Now God's righteousness will cover your heart, placing you in right standing with him, protecting what tries to push its way in and filling you with the Holy Spirit to guide what comes out of your heart.

Not just good news, but wonderful news. It does call for action on your part, though:

> *Above all else, guard your heart,*
> *for everything you do flows from it.*
> —Proverbs 4:23, NIV

That is great advice.

"Follow your heart" or "Guard your heart"? The breastplate of righteousness will guard your heart. But it will not do what God has designed it to do unless you wear it.

Chapter 3

Don't follow your heart. Guard your heart. Put on your breastplate each day.

God's Battle Plan: Growth Point

Guard your heart with the breastplate of righteousness.

God's Reinforcements: Scripture

> *"Above all else, guard your heart, for everything you do flows from it."*
> —Proverbs 4:23 NIV

God's Battle Strategy: Prayer Points

- A heart that devises wicked schemes rests in each one of us. Does this truth surprise you? Why or why not?

- Consider the duties of a guard. How does righteousness (right living) guard and protect your heart?

- Ask God to show you one way to put on your breastplate of righteousness each day.

Notes

CHAPTER 4
Do You Wear Slip-ons or Tie-ons?

IN *KLONDIKE*, THE prospectors must keep alert in front of them and behind them every second or they will discover not just the gold nuggets they have found but their wood and even their stockpiled food stolen. As the relentless winter wears on, Bill Haskell, the series' leading character, is a victim of a theft of his firewood. He beats the thief nearly senseless, but later he decides that in his rush to judgment he did not consider that the man was merely trying to keep his young family warm in the biting cold.

The next morning Bill carries an armload of firewood to the man's cabin. A nice gesture, to be sure, especially after beating the man without first asking why the man would risk stealing his wood. The aftermath of the theft is a good reminder of the human tendency to act first and think later and how trying to remedy a hasty decision may be difficult.

When you think of the word *haste*, what comes to mind? Do you think of "rush," "hurry," or "jump to conclusions"? You may think of others, but would you agree they all suggest an unwillingness to examine a situation until you know the right action to take?

You'll remember in Proverbs 6:16-19, God describes seven sins he hates:

> *There are six things that the Lord hates,*
> *seven that are an abomination to him:*
> *haughty eyes, a lying tongue,*
> *and hands that shed innocent blood,*
> *a heart that devises wicked plans,*
> *feet that make haste to run to evil,*
> *a false witness who breathes out lies,*
>   *and one who sows discord among brothers.*

The Lord starts at the top of the human body and moves down: haughty eyes, a lying tongue, hands that shed innocent blood, a heart that devises wicked plans, *feet that make haste to run to evil,* a false witness who breathes out lies, and one who sows discord among the brethren.

In Paul's letter to the Christians in Ephesus, in Ephesians 6:13-18, God provides a set of practical tools we can use to battle those seven sins:

Take up the whole armor of God, that you may be able to withstand in the evil day, and having done all, to stand firm. Stand therefore, having fastened on the belt of truth, and having put on the breastplate of righteousness, and, as shoes for your feet, having put on the readiness given by the gospel of peace. In all circumstances take up the shield of faith, with which you can extinguish all the flaming darts of the evil one; and take the helmet of salvation, and the sword of the Spirit, which is the word of God, praying at all times in the Spirit, with all prayer and supplication.

Chapter 4

The tools described here help us to fight continually against and overcome the Evil One. When we give no opening to the Evil One to use our head, feet, heart, belly, eyes, ears, or tongue to do what God hates; then the Enemy of our souls is defeated in his perpetual war against us and we are victorious.

To be victorious in our daily walk requires special footwear—shoes for our feet that are designed to lead us toward peace. These shoes are both protective and ready, but not impatient to act—to "open mouth, insert foot" because we were careless and hurried. When we put on these shoes our natural bent to rush into sin is countered by thoughtful, careful preparation. Instead of the default of running to evil, you intentionally choose peace.

Shoes of Readiness

Paul says these shoes have been reinforced by the gospel of peace and are ready for action. The original word for "gospel" in Greek is *euaggelion,* which means "good news" and from which the English word "evangelism," or telling about the good news, comes from. In Paul's time, Roman soldiers wore thick-soled half boots made of strong leather that were tied tightly around the foot. They offered considerable protection, especially for long marches or rough terrain. The soles were thickly studded with short nails, much like today's athletic cleats. The nails provided traction. Strong, well-made shoes readied the soldier for battle and allowed him to endure.

If you have purchased cheap shoes that fell apart within a short time, you know how shoe breakdowns can stop you in your tracks. Women might think of a four-inch high heel breaking off your sole as you are interviewing for a job, while men might think of the sole of a shoe coming unglued while you are walking down the aisle at the start of your wedding. Embarrassing situations, to say the least.

The apostle Paul is referencing shoes that have a lifetime guarantee! These shoes are not flip-flops and do not fall apart with use. In fact, the more you wear them, the more they will mold to your feet. But they will stay stiff and uncomfortable if you accept these shoes but do not wear them. The more you make the gospel of peace a part of your everyday walk, the more it will guide your steps, but if you only occasionally pray or meditate upon the eternal gift God has given, the gospel will not lead you in your everyday life.

Shoes for Defensive and Offensive Battles

A good soldier knows the value of offensive and defensive preparation for battle. Christ-followers, too, prepare for and face a unique battle: we are to "turn from evil and do good; seek peace and pursue it" (Psalm 34:14, NIV). Rather than rush forward into trouble, we are to turn from it (a defensive move)—and then pursue peace with God, peace with others, and peace with ourselves (an offensive move).

Haste can sabotage an operation. That is a hard truth for twenty-first century Christ-followers to learn, and the results of not waiting can be painful. We honk at the car in front of us the instant a light turns green, causing the driver in front of us to get so nervous she almost hits the car in front of her. We roll our eyes and sigh when someone in a check-out line actually writes a check by hand rather than quickly using a debit card, multiplying not just our impatience but that of others in the line.

Maybe it would have been better to think of another alternative. The examples above could lead to clenched teeth and snide comments if we acted from our impatience. The psalm says "turn from evil"—that is a defensive move. Rather than rushing forward into trouble, God wants us to turn away from the temptation to react with haste and anger, being ready to take the pathway of peace instead.

Then, having first decided against the quicker and easier path of lashing out or hitting back, we are to be on the offensive in a way that at first seems illogical but is a model of what Jesus did: We are to "seek peace and pursue it"—peace with God, peace with others, and peace with ourselves.

So these shoes of readiness work both defensively and offensively. Like a Roman soldier's hobnailed boots, nails in your spiritual soles give you stability on any kind of spiritual terrain. When the Enemy or the flesh attacks, you can turn away and avoid slipping, falling or losing traction. Like brakes, these boots prevent you from moving too fast in one direction. Solid footing in God is offensive, too, allowing you to move forward to pursue and impart peace.

EQUIPPED TO WIN

Are Your Shoes Flimsy Slip-Ons or Solid Tie-Ons?

Good equipment is of little use unless you put it on.

That is one reason "feet that are quick to rush into evil" (Proverbs 6:18, NIV) are so abhorrent to God. These feet slip quickly into flimsy shoes—think of lives that are lived without intentionality or out of habit. Rather than constraint governing your behavior, rushing feet become your first impulse, or default mode taking you headlong into trouble. They rely on "internal muscle memory." Hurry proceeds swiftly to harm. Insidious types of sin, like anxiousness, worry, and gossip, which spread quickly, are the result of feet quick to rush into doing, as the old song says, "what comes naturally."

The Bible warns against following our instincts, doing what seems natural to us, or as the previous chapter discusses, following our hearts:

> *The natural person does not accept the things of the Spirit of God, for they are folly to him, and he is not able to understand them because they are spiritually discerned.*
> —1 Corinthians 2:14

We are not "natural people" anymore if we are believers. We are new creations. While our old nature will continue trying to break into our new status, we have a choice of the way to walk our faith journey.

We also have a mandate: to put on the shoes of the readiness of the gospel of peace. The shoes in God's armor require deliberate effort to put them on and tie them.

Chapter 4

You intentionally seek God's way rather than rush into a situation, doing what comes most naturally to you. Once on, they are ready to use. Our feet can then turn away from a flesh default mode or Enemy-induced lure.

Feet shod with the readiness of the gospel of peace are purposeful, ready to press forward with confidence and to impart the peace of God to others, both Christians and nonbelievers.

The gospel of peace is a formidable weapon that helps us not slip or fall when the Enemy attacks us. When we walk in the gospel of peace, we are not easily moved, shaken, or made afraid by the situations we face.

To seek peace, you have to fight for it. You have to arduously go after it and seek to obtain it. It doesn't come by accident. Are you ready?

Over and over Scripture tells us to be prepared, be watchful, be vigilant. When our feet are shod with the readiness of the gospel of peace, we are ready to move defensively away from our natural bent to rush into sin, and move offensively towards Christ-like peace.

God's Battle Plan: Growth Point

God's shoes make you ready for defensive and offensive battles.

God's Reinforcements: Scripture

> *Stand firm ...with your feet fitted with the readiness that comes from the gospel of peace.*
> —Ephesians 6:14-15, NIV

God's Battle Strategy: Prayer Points

- Think about why the desire to hurry is such a temptation. Is it a habit? Is it a feeling of insecurity? Is it a reaction to a fast-paced world? Ask God to teach you patience and persistence—and be prepared to find out that sometimes the best way to learn both is through testing.

- Consider a time when you faced the need to turn away intentionally from attack. Ask God to make you ready to do what he would have you do if a similar situation arises in the future.

- Ask God to give you an opportunity to pursue peace with Him, impart peace to others, or offer peace to yourself.

Notes

CHAPTER 5
Live a Lie or Live the Truth?

"CLICK IT OR ticket."

Have you seen this sign on a major highway as you drive? Some cities have adopted the slogan as a way to remind us to fasten our seat belts. It is an easy way to remember the law.

Yet, in spite of the reminders, non-fatal crash injuries resulted in more than $50 billion in lifetime medical and work loss costs in 2012. Motor vehicle crashes are the leading cause of death among teens.[8] Seat belts save lives, if you wear them.

When we talk about belts what we may picture first are the myriad styles and fabrics used as fashion accessories. But belts also have a valuable role when used for protection. We belt a coat around our waist in cold weather to keep the frigid wind at bay; we put a belt through loops to hold our pants up; we belt-tie several boxes together to keep them from slipping as we move items from one place to another. In short, belts are not just for decoration.

We know that in Proverbs 6:16-19, God describes seven sins he hates, starting at the top of the human body and moving down: haughty eyes, a lying tongue, hands that shed innocent blood, a heart that devises wicked plans, feet that make haste to run to evil, a false witness who breathes out lies, and one who sows discord among brothers.

We also know that Ephesians 6:13-18 lists the tools God provides that we can use to battle those seven sins: the helmet of salvation, the sword of the Spirit, the shield of faith, the breastplate of righteousness, shoes fitted with readiness from the gospel of peace, *the belt of truth*, and prayer.

The belt of truth, cinched around the waist, refers to the same kind of accessory worn by the Romans as they went into battle. This belt was different from today's single-strapped bands we wear around our waist. It had loops on it that would hold the scabbard and other weapons, and it had strips of leather with metal studs embedded in them that hung from the front of it and protected the area of the soldier's body that would allow him to reproduce.

What Do You Reproduce?

We naturally equate reproduction with having children. Yet Scripture points out that we reproduce our thoughts in our actions, behavior, and words: "For as he thinks in his heart, so *is* he." (Proverbs 23:7, NKJV)

What we think is important because we will repeat and act on what is planted in our minds. We have choices to make: we will either agree with God's truth, or we will accept and behave based on the lies of the world, the flesh, and the Devil. God understands that we may struggle to reproduce truth in our lives. Our tendency is to give in to reproducing or repeating the lies of the world, the flesh and our Enemy. When we do that, we become a false witness—because we're not speaking the truth. God helps us overcome this hated sin by giving us the belt of truth to counter the temptation to be a false witness referred to in Proverbs 6.

Telling a Lie or Living a Lie?

We are called to be witnesses, but is our witness true or false? The tool that enables us to be a true witness is the belt of truth. Putting it on, which we must do if we are to use it effectively—gives our consent to Him who is Truth to bind us and control us (holding us in check)—enabling us to refrain from being a false witness by living and speaking lies (what is not true).

Lies stem from pride—we want to have control, or we think we know better, or we want to deceive. Motives for lying are entirely selfish.

When we think of telling lies, our minds naturally go to basic, one-time untruths: "No officer, I didn't realize I was exceeding the speed limit." Or, "No, I didn't spend more during the shopping trip than we agreed." Or even, "Do you know what she did?" (when she didn't). Most of us would agree that telling a lie is an active, deliberate event.

But living a lie can also be passive and can happen almost without notice. It happens when we know something is not true yet we say nothing or overlook it. For example:

- A person witnesses something he or she knows breaks the rules of the community, school, or other group and does not report it. She might as well be telling a lie, because she is not acting when she knows she should.

- Another person may hear a belief someone states that he knows is contrary to what Scripture says. He chooses not to "rock the boat," hoping that someone else will point out the error.

The book of James in the New Testament says this: "Whoever knows the right thing to do and fails to do it, for him it is sin" (4:17). The passive liar chooses to prevent access to the truth or avoid putting it into action instead of doing the right thing.

Here is another example of a passive lie: A witness tells what he has seen or heard without checking the source. By casually accepting a falsehood or passively skimming over it, a false witness denies the truth even though he may not realize it. Once the person has accepted the lie as truth he may feel he must continue the ruse, becoming more active and even embellishing the lie in order to cover his own lack of attention to what he should have verified in the first place.

Then there is the active false witness who deliberately "pours out lies" (Proverbs 6:19 NIV). Think of this analogy: Try to separate out one molecule of water, H_2O, and pour it into a glass. You cannot. The other molecules follow in a stream. Telling falsehoods can turn into a deliberate stream of untruths that follow and follow and follow one after another into the raging waters of deception.

Chapter 5

A sad example of a false witness is the person who becomes so used to living an untruth, so deluded by his lies, that he doesn't realize he's not telling the truth. He may insist even in the face of facts to the contrary that his falsehoods are true.[9] You may have met people you would describe as compulsive liars—you know they are lying, but they don't seem to know.

In other words, a false witness lives a lie by being passive, actively telling untruths, or by living in denial. The lying does not hurt just the liar, who people begin to suspect as untrustworthy—it almost always does great damage to others, as well.

The Belt of Truth Does Not Deny

A false witness is subtle. Your thoughts, behavior, and words that agree with the world, your flesh, or the Enemy are lies. By giving way to them or repeating what is planted in your mind, you deny what God has done for you. In doing so, you give permission for falsehood to reign in your life and become a witness for it. You deny the power of the truth.

You also deny God's transformation in and through you, and that may be the biggest lie of all. When you are ignorant of what God promised because you do not know his Word, you can become susceptible to bogus thoughts: "I am not good enough to be a Christian," "God doesn't love me," and others.

Or you might deny God's transformation in and through you in another way: "I might as well live in sin because I'm already forgiven through Jesus' death and resurrection." Paul warned against this kind of active sin in Romans 6:1-2: "Are we to continue in sin that grace may abound? By no means! How can we who died to sin still live in it?"

The belt of truth will protect you—but you need to know its characteristics. The only way to know them is to know what the Word of God says about you. Here are just a few scriptural truths that reveal not only God's love for you, but His intention for you to live a victorious life:

- John 3:16-17: For God so loved the world, that he gave his only Son, that whoever believes in him should not perish but have eternal life. For God did not send his Son into the world to condemn the world, but in order that the world might be saved through him.

- Romans 8:11: If the Spirit of him who raised Jesus from the dead dwells in you, he who raised Christ Jesus from the dead will also give life to your mortal bodies through his Spirit who dwells in you.

- 2 Corinthians 2:14 (NKJV): Now thanks be to God who always leads us in triumph in Christ, and through us diffuses the fragrance of His knowledge in every place.

- Philippians 4:13: I can do all things through him who strengthens me.

- 2 Timothy 1:7: . . . for God gave us a spirit not of fear but of power and love and self-control.

- 1 John 5:4: For everyone who has been born of God overcomes the world. And this is the victory that has overcome the world—our faith.

- John 14:12: Truly, truly, I say to you, whoever believes in me will also do the works that I do; and greater works than these will he do, because I am going to the Father.

- . . . And many others.

The belt of truth can protect you from reproducing deceptive thoughts. As the belt encircles you, the truth can control your thoughts, behavior, and words, and holds you in check. Since the belt cannot deny the truth, it helps you battle living a lie, allowing you to embrace and access *all* that God has done for you, and what he wants to do in and through you.

When you put on the belt, you are equipped to face the truth . . . and more. You are equipped to victoriously live it out.

God's Battle Plan: Growth Point

Put on God's belt of truth, his Word, to live the truth.

God's Reinforcements: Scripture

> *Stand firm then, with the belt of*
> *truth buckled around your waist.*
> —Ephesians 6:14, NIV

God's Battle Strategy: Prayer Points

- Most of us picture the belt of truth as a tool that points out where we might go wrong. What are some ways the belt can point out what you might omit or deny?

- How can the belt of truth help you agree with God's transformation in and through you?

- Name a time when you denied the truth and how eventually God revealed it to you. Think of others you may know who seem to have believed lies about God. How can you help them learn the truth?

- A belt cinches together other articles of clothing. How does the belt of truth do the same for our hearts?

Notes

CHAPTER 6
Stir Up or Build Up? Putting Your Prayer On

FOR FATHER JUDGE in the *Klondike* miniseries, his armor is his cassock and his crucifix is his shield of faith. He wears them both in all kinds of weather, at all hours of the day and evening, and they seem to be as much a part of him as his wrinkled face. The crucifix is a small item, insignificant to most onlookers. Sometimes it is not even visible because it is under his clerical clothing. Yet his devotion to what the little cross stands for shows in his honorable and righteous behavior. Similarly, there is one piece of our spiritual armor that might not be noticeable to an observer but which underlies every battle a Christian fights. What is it? Can you guess?

In Proverbs 6:16-19, God describes The Hated Seven, starting at the top of the human body and moving down: haughty eyes, a lying tongue, hands that kill, a heart that devises wicked plans, feet that make haste to rush into evil, a false witness who pours out lies, and a man who sows discord among other believers.

Then in Ephesians 6:13-18, God provides a set of practical tools we can use to battle The Hated Seven: the helmet of salvation, the sword of the Spirit, the shield of faith, the breastplate of righteousness, shoes shod with peace, the belt of truth, and prayer.

Have you decided what the remaining tool might be? It is not decorative, as a crucifix can sometimes be, and it's not bright red, as a sash covered with medals and worn across the chest might be. Paul concludes his description of the armor with this urging:

> *And pray in the Spirit on all occasions*
> *with all kinds of prayers and requests.*
> *With this in mind, be alert and always*
> *keep on praying for all the saints.*
> —Ephesians 6:18, NIV

The remaining tool is prayer. The connection between it and the stirring up of discord is clear: both consist of words that come from the mouth, and the mouth pours forth what comes from the heart. They are two ways of communicating that come from our innermost being. Yet the words originate in different attitudes, and they produce altogether different results.

Stir up Discord or Build Up Fellow Believers?

"A man who stirs up discord," or "a person who stirs up conflict in the community," as the NIV in Proverbs 6:19 puts it, speaks up not to state a difference of opinion but rather to create division. His words, or her words, intentionally sow conflict, cultivating and spreading disagreements.

Yet God can use that same mouth to bring blessing on others rather than cultivate strife. If you recognize yourself as one who causes conflict or dissension, how can you change that tendency? Shift your focus away from your needs and wants to praying for others through the direction of the Holy Spirit.

Put Your Prayer On

A believer clothed in God's armor pulls his outfit together with the essential item that enhances the usefulness of the other pieces of armor. That tool is prayer, real prayer, not flowery words that highlight the person's verbal abilities or so-called holiness. It is prayer experienced as a two-way communication between you and God and can be as private as a short request while you brush your teeth in the morning for the Lord to allow you to be a blessing to someone that day. It can also be public prayer expressed with the goal and in the spirit of co-laboring with other believers and with God.

Have you known people who love to participate in public prayer, going on and on in detail about the personal lives of the person they are praying about? Perhaps these sound familiar:

- "Dear God, please help (person's name) with their secret sin of (naming the sin) and help them realize how wrong they are."

- "Dear God, please help (person's or group's name) realize their interpretation of this Scripture (specific doctrine and so on) is wrong."

We might find ourselves chuckling at the examples above. They certainly do not sound like us, do they? Whether they do or not, they illustrate how without listening for the guidance of the Holy Spirit, we may pray for the fulfillment of selfish needs, or we may find ourselves using the framework of group prayer to gossip or badmouth someone.

Words such as these belittle other people and can eventually stir up dissension. These words are not the words of prayer because they focus on oneself, building up the one praying by tearing someone else down.

In contrast, praying in agreement with God's Word and will and empowered by the guidance of the Holy Spirit (Romans 8: 26-27) equips the armor-clad Christ-follower to use his or her words to build up other believers rather than stir up dissension between them. When praying under the guidance of the Holy Spirit, a believer will find it is impossible to sow discord among people.

Be aware that by guiding all you say and do through the filter of prayer, you may find those who oppose you. This is different from using your words or selfish motives to stir up discord, which implies *manipulating, cultivating,* or *working to create disagreements.*

How to Pray to Build Up Fellow Believers

Ephesians 6:18 answers basic questions about how to use this piece of gear:

- Who is praying? You.

Chapter 6

- For whom? For all the saints, all believers in Christ.

- What are you to do? Keep on praying.

- Where should you pray? In the presence of the Holy Spirit.

- When should you pray? On all occasions.

- How should you pray? With alertness and persistence.

There is one more question: Why? Why should you pray? The answer is in Ephesians 6:10: to stand against evil, to "be strong in the Lord and in his mighty power."

When it comes to the content of your prayers for God's people, you can start with Scriptures such as these:

- Pray for mercy: 2 Timothy 1:18a

- Pray for wisdom and revelation: Ephesians 1:16-19

- Pray for spiritual strength: Ephesians 3:14-19

- Pray for purpose: 2 Thessalonians 1:11-12

- Pray for growth: Philippians 1:4-6

- Pray for discernment: Philippians 1:9-11

- Pray for knowledge: Colossians 1:9-12

- Pray for spiritual maturity: Colossians 4:12

When you "put your prayer on" along with the other pieces of armor, you do more than simply avoid conflict. Instead of stirring up others and creating problems among Christ-followers, you build up your brothers and sisters, equipping them to do great things for the kingdom of God. There is no greater pleasure for a believer than to see a fellow Christ-follower receive encouragement to rise to the occasion and step out into battle, confident that the equipment God has provided will be more than sufficient to be able to stand and experience victory over the schemes of the devil.

God's Battle Plan: Growth Point

Put your prayer on. Like a well-fitted garment worn under metal armor, it will be the foundation for the breastplate of righteousness and the shield of faith, providing you with comfort, protection, and endurance.

God's Reinforcements: Scripture

> *And pray in the Spirit on all occasions*
> *with all kinds of prayers and requests.*
> *With this in mind, be alert and always*
> *keep on praying for all the Lord's people.*
> —Ephesians 6:18, NIV

Chapter 6

God's Battle Strategy: Prayer Points

- Describe a time when you have witnessed how words created contention among God's people.

- "When praying in the Spirit, it is impossible to sow discord." How have you seen that truth lived out?

- Ask God to show you one Christ-follower to pray for right now, using the Scriptures listed above. If you have a hard time loving that person, ask the Holy Spirit to reveal to you any selfish attitudes, bitterness, and resentment you may be carrying. Confess those self-centered feelings and ask God to help you demonstrate love and acceptance by your actions.

Notes

CHAPTER 7
Equipped to Win — Love Conquers Hate

AFTER STUDYING THE verses from Proverbs 6 that describe the sins we call "The Hated Seven" and those verses in Ephesians 6 that list the spiritual armor that protects against them, it may still be hard for you to accept that there are things our good God actually hates. You might ask, how can that be?

Before we answer the "how," let us list once more the seven hated behaviors found in Proverbs 6:16-19:

- haughty eyes

- a lying tongue

- hands that kill/shed innocent blood

- a conniving heart/heart that devises wicked plans

- feet that are quick to rush into evil/make haste to run into evil

- a false witness who pours out/breathes out lies

- a man who stirs up discord among brothers/a person who stirs up conflict in the community

Why does God hate these things? If he is Creator over all, did he create these hateful human tendencies?

The answer is this: He did not. Consider Isaiah 53:6:

> *All we like sheep have gone astray; we have turned—every one—to his own way. . . .*

(See also Ezekiel 18:21-32, John 8:34 and Romans 6:16.)

God gave humans the ability to choose to follow him or not. We call that free will—*the power of directing our own actions without restraint or coercion.* God did not make a mistake when he gave each man, woman, and child the choice to go "God's way or their own way." He clearly said, "If you choose my way, you'll have eternal life. If you go your own way, you'll experience death."

Adam and Eve chose to go their own way, imprinting their "I'm my own boss, I call the shots, and I'll manage my own life" DNA into every person that followed after. We are born with this same unredeemed nature that causes us to live in a state of rebellion that separates us from God.

Rebelling against and disobeying the One who made us is wrong. It deserves punishment, would you agree? We need a way to pay for the wrongs we have done against God in order to renew the relationship he designed us to have with him.

Chapter 7

Jesus is the Way

We know God hates certain behaviors because we have just studied The Hated Seven. It is important to also remember this essential truth and engrave it upon our hearts: *He does not hate us.* He will not snub us or refuse to listen to us when we come to him. He created us in his image! Why would a good and perfect God hate what he himself has created?

God in his mercy and love provided redemption through his Son Jesus who took our punishment and died in our place. Because of God's unending love for us, he has provided the way back to him from our choice of the "I'm my own god and I'll do what I please" attitude. More precisely, he has given us *the Way*, using Jesus' own description of himself in John 14:6: "I am the Way, and the truth, and the life. No one comes to the Father except through me." Through Jesus we are able to reestablish fellowship and relationship with him.

Therefore, we can be confident in two eternal truths:

1. His love never fails us even when we fail him:

> *The steadfast love of the L*ORD *never ceases; his mercies never come to an end; they are new every morning; great is your faithfulness.*
> —Lamentations 3:22-23

> *The Lord is not slow to fulfill his promise as some count slowness, but is patient toward you, not wishing that any should perish, but that all should reach repentance.*
> —2 Peter 3:9

2. Because God loves us with an unending, patient, unfailing love, he has provided the means for us to reconcile with him.

God shows his love for us in that while
we were still sinners, Christ died for us.
—Romans 5:8

Jesus Christ, God's Son, was fully human except for the one crucial difference between him and us: He did not sin. While on earth he experienced every temptation we have experienced and continue to experience, but he did not capitulate to those onslaughts of the world, the flesh, and the Evil One. He chose to go God's way and remained One in purpose and mission with his Father.

What was that mission? To be sent by his Father to the world he loved, to substitute himself, spotless and sinless, for each one of us, so we can have a restored relationship with the One who made us. Every single individual, each man, woman, or child, can receive redemption and freedom from their inherited sin nature, by accepting his sacrifice.

That includes you.

Jesus reconciled us to the One who created us, but that is not all: He took the punishment due us for pretending to be our own God when he died in our place. When we accept this free and unearned gift from our Lord, we are declared to be not just "not guilty" but "innocent."

Chapter 7

We become new creatures, spots washed clean and flaws forgiven, in Christ:

> *Therefore, if anyone is in Christ, he is a new creation. The old has passed away; behold, the new has come.*
> —2 Corinthians 5:17

We experience eternal life that begins now—and the best part of this gift is yet to come. Our hearts anticipate experiencing his Kingdom on earth as it is in heaven—a Kingdom that will not end.

Victory over The Hated Seven begins here, but it does not end here. The eternal reward awaits us.

As the apostle Paul exclaimed, "Thank God, who gives us the victory through our Lord Jesus Christ" (1 Corinthians 15:57).

Since we know that through Christ we are victorious, we can confidently press on in spite of the fact there is a spiritual war going on, battles to fight, and temptations to resist. We also know he has not left us defenseless. He has given us the protection we need as we take hold of the battle armor of God.

He has provided all we need to stand strong, to fight, and to win. We may not become rich or see material success in this life. We may experience harsh treatment because of our faith. We may even die for it. But our real fight isn't against people, or a political system, or poverty, or ridicule.

Our real fight is against The Hated Seven, brought to us "compliments of" the Enemy of our souls. But God does not leave us helpless and vulnerable to the schemes of the Enemy.

This book has traced how God equips us to battle the seven sins he hates, giving us everything we need to be victorious over sin and walk in a way that is pleasing to him. You can use the following chart as a reminder to put on the armor God has provided for you and resist the temptation to commit the seven sins he hates.

The Believer's Battle Armor

This piece of armor Ephesians 6:13-18	*Protects you from this sin* Proverbs 6:16-19
Helmet of Salvation	Haughty eyes, lying tongue
Shield of Faith Sword of the Spirit	Hands that kill/shed innocent blood
Breastplate of Righteousness	Conniving heart that devises wicked schemes
Shoes of Readiness Shod with Peace	Feet that are quick to rush into evil
Belt of Truth	False witness, lying tongue
Prayer Guided by the Spirit	Words that stir up dissension and discord

Chapter 7

From Understanding to Acting: A 3-Step Process

1. Understand the Daily Battle.

We need God's armor because we are in a battle every day.

"We . . . wrestle against the spiritual forces of evil" (Ephesians 6:12, ESV). The term used for *wrestle* describes more than an orderly, regulated match on mats. Rather, the original term suggests a violent battle in which the opponents throw one another around with great force, seeking to take each other down. It is hand-to-hand combat . . . and it's that way every day. That makes it continuous—not just a one-time skirmish or challenge. Our fight is an ongoing war.

2. Know the True Enemy.

Who is your true enemy in the war? It is easy to be deceived into thinking your fight is with other people, particularly those who are the recipients of your behavior when you commit the seven sins God hates.

Nevertheless, "we do not wrestle against flesh and blood, but against the rulers, against the authorities, against the cosmic powers over this present darkness, against the spiritual forces of evil in the heavenly places" (Ephesians 6:12 ESV). Clearly, your fight is not against other people ("flesh and blood"). The Enemy isn't even yourself. It is certainly not God.

Your opposition is a team made up of "spiritual forces of evil." They are the "bad guys" who work with Satan, and they use the world and our fleshly desires to influence us and inspire us to do the things that God hates.

Think about this: we won't be battling these "bad guys" in heaven—so this armor is for us to use here, today.

3. Take Up the Armor.

God knows you are vulnerable to temptation. We call these sins "The Hated Seven" because God has listed them for us in the strongest language possible. He doesn't just feel sad about them—he hates them. He despises and abhors them, not because they enable us to have fun and enjoy life without him looking over our shoulder—but because he knows they represent actions that are displeasing to him and debilitate us spiritually. God knows they do great damage to a believer if allowed to become one's typical practice. They give the Enemy a foothold— a position he uses as a base for further advance against us.

God loves you. He understands the daily battle and the war. He knows the Enemy and his army. He knows how to defeat them. He knows what you need in each battle, each day.

God has provided the armor and has equipped you with everything you need to be victorious over the enemy and walk in a way that pleases him.

God gives you what you need to fight. All he asks is for you to recognize and resist your enemies by putting on every piece of your armor . . . and using them in the ways they were meant to be used. Every day.

Chapter 7

God's Battle Plan: Growth Point

Put on the whole armor of God. It's already made to your specific measurements. The more you get used to wearing it, the more natural it will feel.

God's Reinforcements: Scripture

> *"Put on the full armor of God, so that you can take your stand against the devil's schemes. For our struggle is not against flesh and blood, but against the rulers, against the authorities, against the powers of this dark world and against the spiritual forces of evil in the heavenly realms."*
> —Ephesians 6:11-12, NIV

God's Battle Strategy: Prayer Points

- Which piece of armor is one you may forget to put on or think you may not need?

- If you forget that one piece, what do you anticipate might happen? How might it affect the usefulness of the other pieces?

- Think of a time when you may have mistaken your true enemy.

- Over a week or ten days, record the ways God's armor equips you for the daily battles you face.

EQUIPPED TO WIN

This New Testament prayer and encouragement for the early Christians in Hebrews 10:19-23 is also our prayer and encouragement for you:

> *Therefore, brothers, since we have confidence to enter the holy places by the blood of Jesus, by the new and living way that he opened for us through the curtain, that is, through his flesh, and since we have a great priest over the house of God, let us draw near with a true heart in full assurance of faith, with our hearts sprinkled clean from an evil conscience and our bodies washed with pure water. Let us hold fast the confession of our hope without wavering, for he who promised is faithful.*

May the grace and fellowship with our Lord Jesus preserve and empower you until the day of his return.

Notes

A NOTE ABOUT 30 60 100 MINISTRIES

Do you have questions about the principles and truths in this book? Would you like information about the global mission and ministry that spawned this study?

Dalton and Vicki Jantzen are co-founders of 30 60 100® MINISTRIES, INC., a nonprofit organization focused on making common Christian complacency obsolete.

How?

By cultivating a passionate relationship with Jesus, and facilitating spiritual growth and multiplied impact in Christian leaders through leadership development, coaching and training. In a variety of workshops and customized consulting programs 30 60 100® MINISTRIES, INC. equips people of all backgrounds to become effective leaders, build healthy organizations, avoid ministry burn out, and multiply their impact **thirty-, sixty- and one hundredfold**.

30 60 100® MINISTRIES, INC. is about global multiplied

impact. Dalton and Vicki present individualized culturally-sensitive training to leaders throughout North America, Central America, South America, Southeast Asia, Ukraine, and India.

We encourage you to check out the ministry's Web site at **3060100.org.**

We would be delighted to talk with you about getting involved in this growing and dynamic ministry.

Please email us at **dalton@3060100.org** or **vicki@3060100.org** to receive *The Cultivator*, our monthly blog and e-devotional. We will also send you *Faces of the BACK 40,* featuring current stories of Christians around the world.

30 60 100 MINISTRIES, INC.
PO Box 93826
Lubbock TX 79493
806-224-2675 * 505-291-6050

ABOUT THE AUTHORS

Spiritually Healthy Leader®

Vicki Jantzen began her missionary life deep in the jungles of southern Colombia, where she and Dalton helped establish four of the ten mission stations located along a three-hundred-mile span of the Caquetá River.

Vicki is a recipient of the Olsten National Pinnacle Award and is coauthor and facilitator of *The Spiritually Healthy Leader* series of workshops, a leadership-training curriculum designed to equip men and women to become spiritually healthy and finish well on their journey with Christ.

Drawing on their unique ministry and business experience, Vicki and her husband Dalton are cofounders of 30 60 100® MINISTRIES, INC.

On a personal level, Vicki has had to challenge God during some difficult times that most people can only imagine. She explains, "The challenges were not defiant, but needy. We experienced many instances of healing, provision, and protection, such as when terrorist forces attacked our mission station and I had to interact face-to-face with the guerrilla captain. Another time the Colombian government closed the river in an effort to slow the drug traffic. Without any access to supplies, our missionary station's gardens miraculously produced more bounty than ever before, and the station's precious barrel of kerosene did not run out of fuel."

Vicki and Dalton have three grown children and five grandchildren and currently live in Lubbock, Texas.

Dalton Jantzen has more than forty years of experience in leadership, business and ministry formation and transformation, training, coaching, consulting, facilitating, and team leading. He has worked within environments as broadly varied as mining, manufacturing, churches, and parachurch ministries. Dalton has also spent sixteen years together with Vicki in the remote missions outposts of South America.

As a coach to business leaders and owners, he has worked with for-profits and nonprofits, as well as for their boards of directors in both private and public sectors. In the manufacturing world, Dalton has worked with multilingual teams and helped streamline and enhance interactions between teams and their counterparts across borders and competing organizations. Dalton always emphasizes the importance of leading from within, both in the individual and in the organization the person leads.

Fortune 500 companies in the USA, Canada, and Mexico know Dalton through his consulting work with DeLaPorte and Associates, Inc., where he served as senior consultant and special projects leader. His experience and areas of expertise include facilitation, strategic planning, coaching, mentoring, conflict management, production integration, and quality improvement, always with the goal of giving his clients access to "wisdom with heart."

Dalton is a popular speaker and growth cultivator who has instructed groups as well as worked one-on-one with individuals on four continents: Europe, SE Asia, North America, and South America. He is coauthor and facilitator of *The Spiritually Healthy Leader Series*.

Carolyn Stanford Goss is a professional writing coach, stylist, book editor, freelance copy editor, book doctor, ghostwriter, and copywriter. She has done collaborative projects with many authors and has written, cowritten, or ghostwritten several books. She holds a master's degree from Vanderbilt University and has taught English composition, and grammar, drama, developmental reading, and a specialty seminar in the literature of C.S. Lewis at high schools and colleges.

END NOTES

1. The version of the series we refer to is the one that appeared on the Discovery Channel, not the DVD version. The DVD version has edited out several scenes including this one.

2. http://www.zerohedge.com/news/2014-07-25/117-worlds-war-global-geopolitical-risk-mapped

3. http://www.apa.org/topics/divorce

4. http://www.ers.usda.gov/media/1565415/err173.pdf

5. http://www.compassion.com/poverty/poverty.htm

6. http://www.cnn.com/2015/08/04/opinions/trumka-executive-pay/

7. https://www.bannerhealth.com/Services/Health+And+Wellness/Ask+the +Expert/Pediatrics/Is+wearning [sic] +a+helment+that+important.htm

8. http://www.cdc.gov/motorvehiclesafety/seatbelts/facts.html, accessed 10 September 2015.

9. See http://bpdcentral.com/blog/?Why-Do-Narcissists-and-Borderlines-Lie-So-Much, accessed 10 September 2015. The author writes books about people with personality disorders, which is the label many modern counselors, rightly or wrongly, stick on people who habitually lie. She states that often "Some statements may start out as deliberate lies; over time, they become real (the old saying, 'Tell a lie often enough and it becomes the truth')."

Made in the USA
San Bernardino, CA
10 November 2015